three dogs' TALES:

Rescued, Redeemed, and Chosen

SUSAN R. LAWRENCE

Scrivenings
PRESS
Quench your thirst for story.
www.ScriveningsPress.com

Copyright © 2023 by Susan R. Lawrence

Published by Scrivenings Press LLC
15 Lucky Lane
Morrilton, Arkansas 72110
https://ScriveningsPress.com

Printed in the United States of America

All rights reserved. No part of this publication may be reproduced, stored in a retrieval system, or transmitted in any form or by any means—for example, electronic, photocopy, and recording— without the prior written permission of the publisher. The only exception is brief quotations in printed reviews.

Paperback ISBN 978-1-64917-305-8

eBook ISBN 978-1-64917-306-5

Editor: Linda Fulkerson

Cover design by Linda Fulkerson - www.bookmarketinggraphics.com

Scripture quotations are taken from the Holy Bible, New International Version®, NIV®. Copyright © 1973, 1978, 1984 by Biblica, Inc. Used by permission of Zondervan. All rights reserved worldwide.

To all rescue dogs everywhere—with grateful appreciation for your unconditional love.

CONTENTS

PART ONE
RESCUED

Annie's Tale: Rescued	3
Annie the Evangelist	7
Harley and the Sticks	11
Whose House?	15
Don't Go Over the Fence	19
Level Five Aggression	23
A Walk in the Rain	27
Joyful Abandon	31
Extracting a Foot	35
Squirrels in the Grass	39
Our Rescue	43

PART TWO
REDEEMED

Molly's Tale: Redeemed	49
Living Under the Porch	55
The Master's Voice	59
My name is Molly, and I am an Addict	63
A True Friend	67
Give	71
Who's Going Swimming?	75
Don't Eat Poop	79
Deer Bones	83
Moving Boxes	87
Living Redeemed	91

PART THREE
CHOSEN

Maggie's Tale: Chosen	97
Biting the Leash	101
Bridges and Big Things	105
Be Gentle with the Stuffies	109
The Puzzled-Pup Look	113

Wait with Anticipation	117
River of Delights	121
Off-Leash!	125
Outgrowing the Bed	129
Hiking Rules	133
Chosen	137
Author's Note	141
About the Author	143
Also by Susan R. Lawrence	145

Annie's Tale

Rescued

ANNIE'S TALE: RESCUED

THE YELLOW LABRADOR stood knee-deep in water, head drooping from exhaustion. For days she'd been trying to find her way out of the flooded basement. She hadn't eaten, and even though spring had arrived in northeast Iowa, she shivered in the bone-chilling water.

She rarely used her voice, but this was an emergency. Like most Labs, she had a loud, deep bark. A farmer, driving slowly by on the gravel road, heard the dog's anxious cries.

"I heard a dog barking from inside the old Smith place. No one's lived there for years. Might need to see if some dog's trapped in there," the farmer told Webster County animal control.

Shortly after she took the call, Sophia Hubbell and Frank Van Zee entered a driveway where weeds and grass had triumphed over gravel. They walked to the house and opened a door that creaked in protest.

"Here dog, here dog." Frank called, but nothing answered. He and Sophia made their way through the house, shining a flashlight to check under abandoned furniture and in closets. Frank opened a basement door and shone the light down.

The Lab lifted her head and barked one more frantic "woof," as if saying, "Thank God, someone is here."

Frank hurried as fast as he dared on the decrepit stairway. The wave of the dog's tail reassured him of her temperament. He scooped her up. The dog, who should have weighed twenty pounds more, didn't struggle as he carried her to the truck. Frank saw no need to put her in the kennel and laid her on a blanket in the back seat. He sped to the veterinary clinic.

The Lab hovered between life and death. She was emaciated, she'd lost hair from standing in the water, and her legs were covered with cuts and scratches. For two weeks, she remained at the clinic. Slowly, she recovered. As her wounds healed, she gained weight and regrew hair. Her gentle nature endeared her to everyone.

The time came to look for a new home for the Lab. The veterinary staff said goodbye, and she moved to a no-kill animal shelter. They put her picture on Petfinder.com, an internet site to match homeless animals with potential adoptive families.

Across the state, I scrolled through Petfinder. I taught at the local elementary school, but it was July, a good time to introduce a new four-footed friend to our home. The Lab's sweet face stopped my scrolling. I read her story and felt compelled to meet her. I just needed to convince my husband, Gary, who was out of town on business.

At the shelter, they took me to a room lined with cages. When they opened the door of the Lab's cage, she bounded out, came directly to me, sat down, and looked up as if to say, "I've been waiting for you. What took you so long?" I knew instantly she was the dog for me. Sight unseen, my husband named her Annie.

Annie adjusted easily to her brand-new life. She romped and explored the five wooded acres where we lived. She slept on a soft, comfy dog bed. In the family room, a basket held toys just for her. She had food in the pantry and a jar of special treats on the counter.

I dreamed of Annie accompanying me in my classroom. So, we went to obedience school, where she learned to sit, stay, and come. She completed three classes and qualified as a Canine Good Citizen. Next, she took Therapy Dogs International's test and passed with only a slight hesitation when she walked by the treats on the floor. I now owned a therapy dog.

The school board members were skeptical when I asked permission to bring my dog into the classroom. "You already have students prone to distraction. How will they react to a dog running around the classroom? And we may be opening ourselves up to a lawsuit."

I reassured them the certifying therapy-dog organization provided insurance. Finally, they agreed to a trial. I could bring her one day a week for the two months of school remaining—if there were no incidents of misbehavior.

Annie took to our new routine as if she'd been bred for this life. We rose early and walked before we hopped into the car for the trip to the school. After all, she was barely two years old and still had lots of energy. Annie somehow knew her purpose in the classroom. When the children entered, she greeted each one. She lay on the floor as students read to her, showed her math work, or whispered secrets. If I had supervision duties at recess, Annie went outside, and students from all the classes lined up to walk her around.

For the three years until my retirement, Annie worked alongside of me. After the two-month trial, the school board okayed Annie as the mascot of Room 419, and she accompanied me every day school was in session. She participated in assemblies, fire drills, and school parties. Her school ID was attached to her vest, and on special days, she wore a Character Counts T-shirt. She was pictured in the elementary yearbook. The entire school, from janitors to the principal, saw Annie as an integral part of the community.

Annie never had favorites among the children, but she somehow understood if a child needed her comforting strength. This special gift manifested even more after my retirement. We took on a volunteer job at Orchard Place, a school for children with behavioral disorders and mental illnesses.

When we arrived, Annie walked into the classroom and made her way past every desk, pausing at each for a pat. Then she would choose one desk to sit by. Often, the child she chose was having a difficult day.

Dillon, an outgoing young man, spent one-on-one time with Annie each week. He spent as much time visiting with me as he did playing with Annie. One day the staff called on the house phone. "Dillon is having a rough time. He won't be coming for his session with Annie."

I gathered up Annie's toys, but the phone rang again. "Dillon really wants his time with Annie. We've decided to let him come."

When Dillon trudged into the room, the evidence of his "rough time" showed—red, teary eyes, his whole body slumped and bowed down. He barely acknowledged my presence and stretched out on the floor beside Annie. For the next hour, Dillon talked to Annie, whispering into her silken ears.

His therapist told me later that Dillon said of the visit, "Annie saved me."

The rescued dog now rescued children.

ANNIE THE EVANGELIST

I RECOGNIZED the power of Annie's rescue story. And so did others. I began telling the story at churches around Iowa. Annie always accompanied me, and she delighted and entertained audiences with her routine of tricks.

Annie loved meeting people, especially children. However, Annie didn't always act like a proper evangelist. At home, she couldn't be trusted—she chewed books to shreds and tore pillows open, leaving piles of stuffing all over. Any food within her reach was fair game. Annie remembered starving. Leave a cookie on the coffee table, and she would be licking her lips when you returned.

But her worst misbehaviors occurred when we walked in the woods. Annie found any dead animal within sniffing range. Now I am not talking just a little dead, but really dead—reeking-of-odor dead. And then she rolled in it. Not just a once-over. She spun this way and that and rubbed the *eau-de-decay* onto her shoulder and a bit behind her ear and then all the way to the tip of her tail.

"Oh, Annie," I gasped as she bounced up to me. I tried to avoid her, tried to breathe through my mouth, tried just to get a breath without gagging. "Evangelists don't roll in dead things!"

Then I thought—all Christians are called to be evangelists. Do I ever roll in dead things? Oh, I don't mean lie down on the ground and rub my back over a dead possum in the field. But do I do or say things offensive to people who need to hear about Jesus?

In 2 Corinthians, Paul describes Christians as the *aroma of Christ.* Do I exude the aroma of Jesus? The aroma of life? I wonder if I smell like Jesus when I argue. I wonder if I smell like Jesus when I'm unkind to others. I wonder if I smell like Jesus when I gossip about other people.

Annie never knew when she would accompany me to a school or church or retreat. I did my best to keep her from rolling on dead animals because instead of children wrapping their arms around Annie and saying, "I love this dog!" there would be a whole chorus of "Yuuuck!" and "Ew!"

We never know who is watching or listening to us, either. It might be someone who doesn't know Jesus. If we're doing offensive things, they never smell that sweet fragrance of Jesus, which is everlasting life. We may be their only chance to see or meet or know Jesus. Let's not blow it by rolling in dead things.

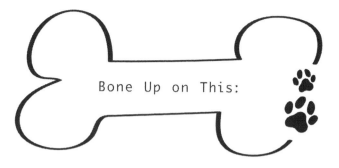

For we are to God the aroma of Christ among those who are being saved and those who are perishing. To the one we are the smell of death; to the other, the fragrance of life.

2 Corinthians 2:15-16

Lord, help me to be the carrier of Your fragrance to others.

HARLEY AND THE STICKS

ANNIE'S best friend in all the world was a squatty, brown boxer named Harley. Harley lived two houses away. When she heard Annie and me, she would come running down the lane so she could walk with us. Whenever Harley appeared, Annie became a leaping, tail-wagging bundle of excitement. They greeted each other with sniffs and kisses. Then they walked together, sharing every good smell and interesting clump of grass.

Sticks, however, were not shared. Both Harley and Annie loved to chase sticks. When I threw one, they barreled across the yard, grabbed it in their strong jaws, and eventually brought it back to me. If Harley and Annie happened to reach a stick at the same time, they both seized an end. Annie went one direction; Harley went another. Two equally strong dogs at an impasse. Neither dog could move forward until one gave up.

Sometimes we are like Annie and Harley in our relationships. Whether it is family, work, or church, we often grab hold of something and try to keep it all to ourselves. It might be an idea of how something should be done or control over a certain situation. We hold that "stick" and refuse to give in to the person on the other end of our disagreement. As a result, we are stuck in the same place, and nobody wins. Just like Annie and Harley, we hold opposite ends of the stick and cannot move forward.

Working together is a behavior that pleases God. Sometimes we need to simply let go of the stick and let the other person carry it. Sometimes we need to work out a compromise and carry it together. However we work it out, it should be done with unity.

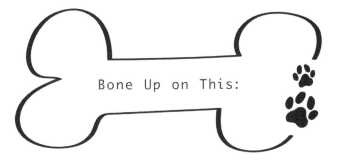

How good and pleasant it is when brothers live together in unity!

Psalm 133:1

Lord, help me to work in unity with others to accomplish Your purpose.

WHOSE HOUSE?

ANNIE LOVED THE RAIN. She never missed an opportunity to dip in a puddle. First, she put one foot in, then she splashed, and finally, she lay down in the middle with what appeared to be a grin on her face. After an early spring walk, mud wedged between her toes in little balls, covered her feet and legs in a solid coating, and splotched her belly with globs. Even her persistently wagging tail was fringed with mud. In exasperation, I looked at her and asked, "Whose house are you going to sleep in tonight?"

We both knew I joked. I patiently sprayed water from the hose to clean off every particle of mud, then toweled her feet, legs, and belly dry. She bounded into the house and stretched out on whatever rug she chose for her after-walk snooze.

Just like Annie, we accumulate mud. No matter how hard we try, while we're here on earth, we continue to disobey God. It might be our refusal to forgive an offense that becomes a mud ball of bitterness wedged between our toes. Maybe we worry, not trusting God to be in control, and then our body is splotched with the mud of fear. Or perhaps we just become cynical, and our "tail"—the part of us that communicates—is fringed with the mud of negativity when we should be uplifting.

Who may ascend the hill of the Lord? Who may stand in His holy place? He who has clean hands and a pure heart.

Psalm 24:3-4

What a blessing to know however much mud we accumulate, God never asks us, "Whose house are you going to?" His word assures us He has the power to give us the "clean hands" necessary to enter His house. When temptations, our stubborn will, and our sinful nature cover us with ugly mud, all we need to do is sincerely confess those sins. He lovingly and patiently cleans us with the blood of Jesus. Our invitation to His house, as part of His family, is forever.

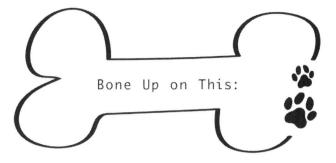

If we confess our sins, He is faithful and just and will forgive us and purify us from all unrighteousness.

1 John 1:9

Lord, help me be slow to dip my toes in the mud and quick to ask forgiveness when I do.

DON'T GO OVER THE FENCE

WHEN ANNIE and I walked in the woods and fields, I kept her close. Her Lab nose and strong legs could carry her far away and into unanticipated dangers. A crumpled wire fence marked the boundary between the tilled land and the dense timber beyond. Annie's nose went up as we approached.

"Don't go over that fence," I warned. She eyed me as if she were weighing the consequences. Her nose went higher, catching on the breeze the tantalizing scents from the woods—squirrels, birds, possums, and more.

"Annie, don't go over the fence," I repeated as I kept walking. But when I looked back, Annie hopped over and buried her snout deep in the grass. I turned back to get her, scolding as I went, "Don't you listen? Didn't you see that fence? You will only get into trouble over there."

God sets boundaries for us too. His Word, the Bible, clearly lays them down. The Ten Commandments and the Golden Rule are perhaps the most familiar, but every book, every chapter includes instructions. We also have boundaries in our communities: laws on how fast we can drive our cars, where we can walk, and how much of our money we are to give to the government.

When we contemplate crossing one of the boundaries, God warns us. The warning may come in His Word, from a sermon or an article we read, or even the counsel of a godly friend. If we listen to the warning and don't cross the boundary, we take the path of obedience.

God's laws and community laws are there to protect us, whether we agree with them or not. Crossing a boundary always has consequences.

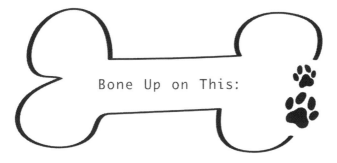

It is the Lord your God you must follow, and Him you must revere. Keep His commands and obey him; serve Him and hold fast to Him.

Deuteronomy 13:4

Father, what boundaries have I been stepping over? Give me the strength today to walk on Your path of obedience.

LEVEL FIVE AGGRESSION

WE NEVER KNEW who we would meet when Annie and I volunteered at Orchard Place, the school for children with behavioral and mental health disorders. When Katelyn skipped into the room, I was momentarily taken aback. Most of the residents were teenagers. This chubby-cheeked little girl appeared to be seven or eight.

She immediately began petting Annie and bombarding me with questions. "What's her name? Why is she here? Does she like kids?" I answered each question the best I could.

Katelyn poked a finger into Annie's mouth. "Does she bite?" Perhaps the sharp, white teeth intimidated the young girl.

"No, she doesn't bite," I answered.

Annie stood patiently, her tail wagging, as Katelyn continued examining every part of the dog. "Does she bite?" she asked again. I paused, confused as to why she would repeat the question.

"When I bite, it's level-five aggression." Katelyn stared at me as she pulled Annie's ear.

I moved her hand and modeled stroking. "She doesn't bite, but we want to be gentle with her so we don't hurt her."

Katelyn had no fears of Annie biting—she feared *she* might bite the dog!

I've never had my aggressions numbered in intensity, but I certainly do bite sometimes. I snap at my children for some minor infraction. I argue with my husband. I am unkind and selfish, especially when others irritate me.

Any time I don't use my words to lift, encourage, and comfort others, it should be called a level-five aggression.

We all could take a lesson from Annie, who never bit, but stood patiently, always loving, always kind—even when children poked and pulled her ears.

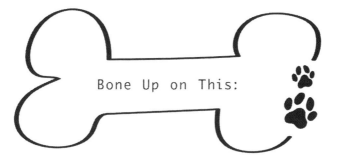

Reckless words pierce like a sword, but the tongue of the wise brings healing.

Proverbs 12:18

Father, may my words bring healing to others today.

A WALK IN THE RAIN

THE TEMPERATURE READ FORTY DEGREES, and a cold rain turned the spring morning gray. Annie didn't care. She couldn't read the thermometer, and she loved rain.

I ignored her nudges and pacing for at least an hour, but the rain showed no signs of letting up. So, I layered raincoat over warm coat over sweatshirt and stepped outside. I only intended to go to the end of our driveway, but Annie was delighted with the wet world. She danced through puddles, rolled in rain-soaked grass, and returned to laugh up at me. Her entire body seemed to shout, "Isn't this great? Thanks for bringing me out!" We ended up going for a long walk and returning soaked, but happy. Giving pleasure to Annie filled me with joy too.

Matthew 7:12 (the Golden Rule) is usually used as a warning (mostly to children) that we should not be unkind to others because we would not want others to be unkind to us. I think Jesus wanted us to think beyond that interpretation.

When we sacrifice our time, money, or talents to bring pleasure to others, we treat them as we want to be treated. This might mean we go to a football game with our husband (even when we don't know a first down from a field goal) because it brings him pleasure. Or we lie on the floor and play Legos with our four-year-old, although we have a lengthy list of things to do. Maybe we watch a movie with our teenagers, just to spend some time with them. Like a walk in the rain on a cold March morning, treating others as we would want to be treated is often difficult but almost always fills us with the blessing of joy.

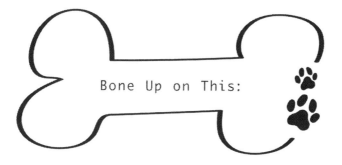

In everything, do to others what you would have them do to you.

Matthew 7:12

Lord, help me not only do *to* others, but do *for* others, blessing them with what brings them joy.

JOYFUL ABANDON

THE WATER-LOVING gene in Labradors is completely unaffected by the water's temperature, location, or even its clarity. While we walked one early spring morning, Annie spotted a ditch filled with melting snow. With joyful abandon, she plunged in, leaping and frolicking, dipping her head under and out, and splashing water everywhere. The water must have been frigid and filled with winter debris. But Annie didn't stop to consider anything but the joy of swimming.

God created Annie with a love of water. He created you with talents and gifts He wants you to use for His purpose and glory. Too often, we fret over our gifts—*I'm not good enough; This is too much work; I'm not qualified; I'm too old for this*—rather than letting it bring us joy.

How pleasing to God if we leap into life with Him like Annie leaps into water. If you're certain God has called you to do something, you don't have to fear the "location" or the "temperature." Trusting in Him, you can fully rely on His strength and His promise that He will give you all that is needed to complete His work. With joyful abandon, plunge into whatever adventures God has for you.

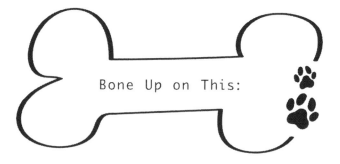

Whatever you do, work at it with all your heart, as working for the Lord, not for men, since you know that you will receive an inheritance from the Lord as a reward. It is the Lord Christ you are serving.

Colossians 3:23-24

Lord, help me serve You with joyful abandon.

EXTRACTING A FOOT

ONE WARM SUMMER DAY, Annie and I walked a long distance from the house. I glanced down and noticed she wasn't beside me. I turned around and saw her lying down and vigorously chewing on something. Annie often found old bones on our walks. I could usually convince her to leave them. This time, however, my command to "drop it" didn't result in compliance.

I went back to see what she was chewing on and whether or not I could extract it. Annie obediently opened her jaws, and when I reached in, I was horrified. She held a foot in her mouth. Something had killed and eaten a badger or groundhog, and Annie found the remains—a foot complete with claws.

After I finished gagging, I stopped to think of how often I am required to extract a foot. Usually, it's mine, inserted into my mouth because I didn't think before I spoke. The Bible addresses this malady.

The tongue also is a fire, a world of evil among the parts of the body ... All kinds of animals, birds, reptiles, and creatures of the sea are being tamed and have been tamed by man, but no man can tame the tongue. It is a restless evil, full of deadly poison.

James 3:6-8

How true this is! When we engage our mouths before we think, we can be unkind, thoughtless, and cruel. Our words become weapons, wounding others. Is there nothing we can do? Are we stuck with this uncontrollable part of our body? Absolutely not. As Christians, we have the power of Christ living in us. We can exert control. I think we need to note here, "the tongue" also applies to what we write—especially in social media.

A good way to control our tongues is to pray before we speak or write, especially in tense situations. Annie had the choice when she saw the badger's foot—she could scoop it up in her mouth or pass it by. And we have a choice every time we open our mouths—we can use words with the power to encourage, inspire, or heal—or we can put that rotting badger foot in.

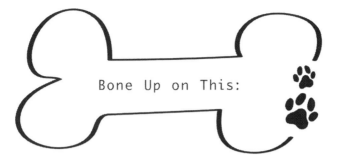

Everyone should be quick to listen, slow to speak, and slow to become angry.

If anyone considers himself religious and yet does not keep a tight rein on his tongue, he deceives himself, and his religion is worthless.

James 1:19,26

Lord, help me to use my words to heal, not to harm.

SQUIRRELS IN THE GRASS

ANNIE ATTENDED OBEDIENCE SCHOOL. She learned to sit, lie down, and, most importantly, how to walk quietly by my side. Most of the time, Annie walked calmly in the heel position. But one thing lured her away every time—squirrels.

When Annie spotted a squirrel, she couldn't resist. Tail waving madly, she ran flat-out across the yard in pursuit. The squirrel, of course, scurried up the nearest tree and looked down, scolding Annie with high-pitched chattering.

If I needed Annie's complete attention, I needed to plan a route that bypassed squirrels.

I am a follower of Jesus Christ. He commands me to walk with Him, to be yoked with Him. But, like Annie, I have my "squirrels" that lure me away from my Master's side. Busyness can keep me so consumed with what I consider my "must-dos" that I don't take time to connect with Him in prayer and in the Word. Sometimes I spend hours on mindless diversions—social media, computer games, solving puzzles—hours that could be devoted to kingdom work.

What squirrels are in your grass? What lures you away from God's side?

Just like I did for Annie, we need to make plans for our lives to evade those familiar temptations.

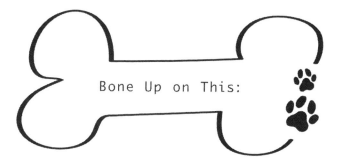

No temptation has seized you except what is common to man. And God is faithful; he will not let you be tempted beyond what you can bear. But when you are tempted, he will also provide a way out so that you can stand up under it.

1 Corinthians 10:13

God, keep me from chasing after the squirrels that prevent me from following You.

OUR RESCUE

EVEN MORE AMAZING than Annie's rescue, is our own story of Jesus's rescue of us.

Just like Annie, we are trapped in an old house. The house is made up of sin—everything we do or say or even think that is wrong or against God's laws. Sin separates us from God. All our attempts to reach God with our own power are as futile as Annie's attempts to free herself. We can try our best to be good, to do the right things, but we always fail.

The shelter staff sent Frank to rescue Annie. The One sent to rescue us is God's own Son, Jesus Christ.

For God so loved the world that he gave his one and only Son, that whoever believes in him shall not perish but have eternal life.

John 3:16

Jesus never sinned, yet He suffered and died on the cross to rescue us. After three days He arose, and now He is seated at the right hand of God and intercedes for all who believe in Him.

When we ask, He reaches down and pulls us out of that pit of sin and into a brand-new life with Him. Annie led a brand-new life. She lived with my husband and me, went to schools and churches, and participated in a wonderful ministry. In our new lives, we belong to the family of God. We have the promise of eternal life. And we have the great joy of living to serve Him.

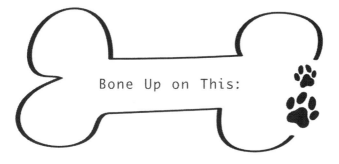

Bone Up on This:

He lifted me out of the slimy pit, out of the mud and mire; he set my feet on a rock and gave me a firm place to stand. He put a new song in my mouth, a hymn of praise to our God. Many will see and fear and put their trust in the Lord.

Psalms 40:2-3

Lord, help me to live as one who has been rescued to serve.

Molly's Tale
REDEEMED

MOLLY'S TALE: REDEEMED

A TINY GOLDEN-HAIRED puppy squirmed in the dirt beneath the porch. In the house above her, the noise of people sounded far away and muffled—not really a part of her world. She nursed, wrestled with her twelve siblings, slept, and grew while her mother scrounged for food in the surrounding countryside.

The puppies were a combination of short and long-hair, lanky and stubby legs, and floppy and lop ears. The golden puppy had the broad body of her Labrador mother and the short, knobby legs of a Corgi. Cautious by nature, she always peered out to survey the landscape before venturing from under the porch. She never interacted with the people as her siblings did. But if the dogs played tag, she led the pack.

When their mother's milk dried up, they all ate dry food the people sporadically poured into a dirty dish. They never had enough, and their small tummies cramped with hunger. The puppies traveled farther from home in search of something to eat.

Then they found the neighboring farmer's chicken house. The chickens squawked and flapped their wings, so the puppies chased them, grabbing feathers from their tails. The golden puppy seized a chicken by a leg. Like children at a dessert table, they shoved and pushed to get the warm dinner. Suddenly, a sharp bang startled them away. Several more reports followed.

The farmer had used his shotgun to protect his property. The puppies fled in terror, but four of them lay dead in the dirt. When the mother dog's owner realized what happened, she, at last, did something responsible—she called the animal shelter.

The shelter volunteers arrived the next morning in a van. They scooped up puppies and put them in carriers. The two mama dogs barked, puppies ran everywhere, and the people from the house shouted. The golden puppy crouched under the porch and watched. When someone reached for her, she bolted. She flattened herself out and raced across the yard, weaving around and between the people. No one could catch her.

The volunteers promised to come back the next day for the remaining puppies and drove off with the captured ones, safe in carriers. The golden puppy hid in the field, trembling. When darkness surrounded the house, she crept back and crawled to her bed in the dirt.

The next day the volunteers returned, and after a mad scramble, they trapped the puppy under the porch and caught her at last. They called her Shylo because of her cautious nature.

As they prepared her for adoption, Shylo learned about regular meals, loving touches from a person, and wearing a collar and leash. After two weeks, the shelter posted pictures of the puppies on Petfinder.

My husband Gary and I had buried Annie six months earlier after she had succumbed to a short bout with cancer. We grieved her loss. Gary didn't want another dog. But I couldn't bear the empty spaces where a dog had been—in my home and in my heart. I opened the Petfinder website again.

I paused when I spotted the perky puppies with bright eyes. A description accompanied each puppy featured in the photos. In the background, always partially hidden behind her brothers and sisters, I spied Shylo. But for several days, she wasn't featured or given a description. I thought, "What about the golden puppy?"

Finally, her picture and a short account were posted. I called the shelter and made an appointment to meet her. When I arrived, a group of dogs ran to the edge of the fenced enclosure to greet me—wagging tails, jumping, and barking. Shylo stood at the back of the yard, gazing intently at me with dark eyes.

The shelter director met me outside and led me to an area for prospective adopters and dogs. Then she brought Shylo and one of her siblings, Kookie, into the yard. Kookie immediately leaped into my lap, wagging her tail and showering me with kisses. Shylo watched, just out of reach. After a time, she allowed me to pet her. Confident I could win her trust, I told the shelter director I would take Shylo home.

The two puppies followed us inside. Shylo immediately crawled under a desk and hid. I signed the papers to make her ours, pulled her out from her hiding spot, and put her in a carrier in the back of my car. Without a whimper or a bark, she pressed against the back of the kennel and watched me through terrified eyes.

We drove the twenty minutes to our acreage, where I discovered her terror had caused her to mess in the kennel. I carried her into the house and cleaned her up as best I could. She found a dark corner behind the couch where she felt safe. She came out briefly to eat and drink before returning to her spot. Gary renamed her Molly, and I hoped she could soon shake her shy identity.

The next day she let Gary and me pet her, and she chose a place on the couch instead of behind it. The foster family had done an excellent job teaching Molly to use the grass for her bathroom. I took her on a leash to the long grass at the edge of the yard and, within a week I pronounced her "housebroken." But she was far from being a well-trained house dog.

One night shortly after Molly came, we went out for the evening. We returned after only a few hours to find she had chewed her way out of the hard-sided kennel we'd left her in and made her way to the basement, where she had torn up several things, furiously scratched a closed door, and left messes in several places. I held the terrified puppy until she calmed and fell asleep.

We bought a wire cage so she could see out when kenneled, and, after we learned to clip it together at every seam, she seemed to tolerate it.

As the months went by, the list of things Molly destroyed grew longer: a computer power cord, two Fitbits, multiple books, several articles of clothing, leashes, my granddaughter's expensive headband, and more items I've mercifully forgotten. Although we were careful to crate her when we left the house, when we were at home, she quietly disappeared into a room and snatched something off a nightstand or a counter.

When she was seven months old, we took a car trip to Texas. We stayed at a friend's home for a few days, then traveled to a motel in Galveston. While we were traveling, we needed to stop frequently to walk Molly. If we left her alone in the car, she found something to destroy—like a seatbelt or her leash or water bottles. One time she tore open a bag of rice I had just purchased. Rice was buried in the carpet throughout the car. When we got to our motel, we wanted to rest. Molly tore around, up on the bed and off, into the bathroom and out. The frigid winter air made it difficult to walk her as much as she needed. *Molly, No* seemed to be her name.

Back home, I took her to obedience classes, and she passed the test to become a Canine Good Citizen. She grew less destructive. But for the rest of her life, she could not be off the leash, or she would lead us on a wild chase. We needed to watch carefully what items—especially food—were within her reach. And she remained frightened of all strangers. But despite the challenges she presented, we grew to cherish Molly. With us, she wagged, kissed, and cuddled, her shyness gone. She loved hiking and camping with me, even completing one hundred miles of the Appalachian Trail. And she gradually added each of our close friends to her circle of trust.

From a wild puppy who destroyed anything in her path to a mostly well-mannered dog who brought us laughter and love, Molly's life had been redeemed.

He brought me out into a spacious place, He rescued me because He delighted in me.

Psalm 18:19

LIVING UNDER THE PORCH

WHEN MOLLY FIRST CAME HOME, she exhibited an odd habit—she ate all her meals lying down. The high-energy puppy watched while I poured food into her dish. Then she dropped to the floor and lay with the bowl between her paws. She proceeded to crunch away on her food but didn't stand until the dish was licked clean.

Our spacious kitchen provided Molly her own spot to eat with a mat and large ceramic bowls. But after living in the cramped quarters under the porch where she was born, this was the only way she knew to eat.

If we gave her food from our hands, held the dish up, or put it on the footstool, she stood. But for many weeks, if we let her choose, she lay down to eat. She clung to the old habit, even though she no longer lived under the porch.

If we know Jesus, we live a new life with Him. We live in a spacious place, an eternal life, a life filled with the power of the Holy Spirit. But sometimes we act like we still live under the porch. We hold onto habits formed before we were living the Christian life.

Are you clinging to habits of your old life? Lift up your head. Look at the spacious rooms God has prepared for you. Then do what is needed to cast those old habits aside.

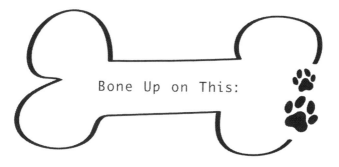

Bone Up on This:

Therefore, if anyone is in Christ, he is a new creation, the old has gone, the new has come!

2 Corinthians 5:17

God, help me have the strength to break old habits and live in Your spacious rooms.

THE MASTER'S VOICE

MOLLY RECEIVED A NEW NAME, a new home, and a new life when she came from the shelter. She loved the regular meals, belly rubs, and long walks. Some of our house rules, not so much. But she worked hard to learn the language. She quickly understood "treat" and "walk" and "sit." It took longer for her to learn "Don't chew that" and "Go in your kennel."

The more time she spent with my husband and me, the more words she learned. Walking beside us, lying at Gary's feet in the family room, watching me in the kitchen—she soaked in the language and began to understand her new life.

When we have received new life in Christ, we have a Master's voice we need to hear and understand too. And, just like Molly, the more time we spend with our Master, the more we understand what He has to say to us.

When we read and study His word, talk with Him in prayer, and quiet our hearts to listen for His voice, the sometimes-confusing world of being a Christ follower will become more familiar, more understandable. We will begin to know our Father's language.

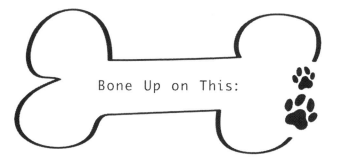

The man who enters by the gate is the shepherd of His sheep ... He calls His own sheep by name and leads them out. When He has brought out all His own, He goes on ahead of them, and His sheep follow Him because they know His voice.

John 10:2-4

Lord, help me to spend time with You, so I can know and understand Your voice.

MY NAME IS MOLLY, AND I AM AN ADDICT

MOLLY WAS A TISSUE-AHOLIC. She couldn't resist them. Used, unused, nearly disintegrated from being in a pocket—it didn't matter, she loved them. Regardless how well we hid them, she would find the delicious morsel. A cute, lidded wastebasket I bought to keep her out? She flipped it open with her nose. Tucked down in my pocket? She sniffed the tissue out and nuzzled her way in to gain the treasure.

Once she had a tissue, she shredded it, mouthed it until it was soggy, and maybe even ate it, depending on her mood. What she wouldn't do was release it. If you pried her mouth open, she held it between her back teeth or under her tongue. Yes, she was an addict. She loved tissues and refused to change.

Maybe you're not addicted to tissues like Molly was (*I hope not!*), but everyone has a few addictions they prefer to keep hidden. After a nearly life-long battle with my weight, I can't deny I'm addicted to food. It doesn't have the negative effects of a drug, such as meth, but I am still depending on something to bring pleasure or comfort other than the only One who can fill the empty parts in me.

What addiction are you struggling to overcome today? Listen to the words of the Psalmist and make it your prayer.

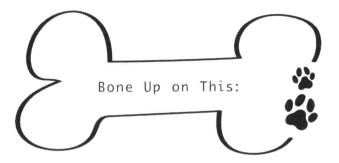

Whom have I in heaven but you? And earth has nothing I desire besides you. My flesh and my heart may fail, but God is the strength of my heart and my portion forever.

Psalm 73:25-26

God, give me the strength to let go of my addictions and turn to You, and only You, to satisfy.

A TRUE FRIEND

EVERY MORNING, Molly stood at the door watching for her friend Teddy, who lived over the hill and through the woods. He came to the back door daily, begging for her to come out and play. Teddy, a gorgeous golden retriever, weighed close to one hundred pounds. His size didn't intimidate Molly a bit. He played the way she loved—wrestling, rolling, running, and play biting.

Molly raced outdoors and ran in giant circles around him. Teddy tried gallantly to catch her, lumbering his bulk across the yard. Eventually, he plopped down, exhausted. Molly danced around him, rushing in to nip at his ears, legs, and tail, enticing him to continue playing. When Teddy had enough, he simply straddled her, sat his bulk on top of her, and put her head in his mouth. He never hurt her—he just let her know she'd crossed the line.

Do you have a friend who will sit on you if you cross the line? Maybe not literally, but a friend who holds you accountable in your Christian walk? Friends who will do that are invaluable if we are to become all God intends.

If you don't have someone who will pray with and for you, tell you if you are gossiping or being unkind, and continually encourage you in your spiritual walk—reach out to someone. Ask them if they'll take the time to pray with you weekly. Share your needs—spiritual and otherwise. And praise God for them when they sit on you!

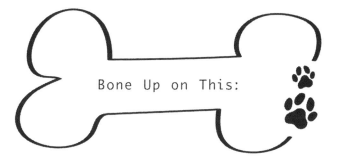

As iron sharpens iron, so one man sharpens another.

Proverbs 27:17

God, thank you for friends who care enough about me to give godly counsel, even if means they sit on me.

GIVE

AS MOLLY GREW, so did the temptations inside the house. When things were quiet, Gary and I looked around. If we didn't see her, we knew she was off thieving. In addition to tissues, she loved socks, dryer sheets, Gary's handkerchiefs, and the grandkids' small plastic toys. She'd lived with us long enough to know she would be in trouble if she chewed one of these temptations. So, whenever we were occupied, she'd sneak off to another room, looking for something within reach to steal.

We taught her "leave it" and "not yours," and she improved. After a while, I even left the bedroom doors open. One day, I decided to test her training. Gary had left socks on the floor of the family room (yes, I know, he needs training too), so, I handed Molly one of the socks and said, "Carry."

Head high and tail wagging, she proudly trotted after me into the bedroom and up to the hamper. But when I commanded, "Give," we had a bit of trouble. She wanted to chew that delicious sock and not give it back to me. I grabbed for it, and Molly took off on a chase around the house. When I finally retrieved the sock, it was ragged and soggy.

Everything we have has been given to us by God's gracious hand—

our talents and abilities, our treasured time, and even our loved ones. Why, then, do we hold so tightly to what He asks us to give?

If we acknowledge God as our Lord, we need to be ready to freely and openly part with anything we have—before it is ragged and soggy. He may allow us to "carry it," but we must be ready to "give" when He asks.

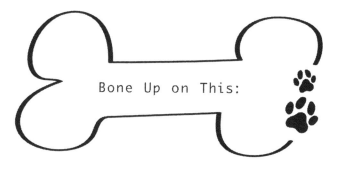

Freely you have received, freely give.

Matthew 10:8

Father, thank you for all You have given me. May I give freely when You ask.

WHO'S GOING SWIMMING?

WHEN MOLLY'S best friend Teddy came over the hill toward our house, Molly went into a frenzy of excitement.

If I let her out, they wrestled, ran, and played. Then, they headed toward Teddy's house, because he had the World's Best Playground for a Lab—a pond in his front yard. Hours later, Molly would return, exhausted, muddy, and full of burrs.

Teddy meant well—he just wanted a playmate. But when Molly was with him, she always ended up wet and filthy. Then she had to endure a scrub in the tub and a long burr-picking session before being allowed inside again.

Sometimes, we have people like that in our lives. They come over the hill, and before we know it, we're engaged in all sorts of behaviors we shouldn't—a bad habit we promised to break, gossiping, telling off-color jokes, or perhaps descending into a negative mindset. The people are not really to blame—we're the ones who choose to follow them into the muck and mire.

If Molly stayed in our yard, she wouldn't get so muddy. But she chose to follow Teddy (or lead him!) into the pond.

When we're with others, in spite of what they are saying or doing, let's be certain all of our speech and actions glorify God.

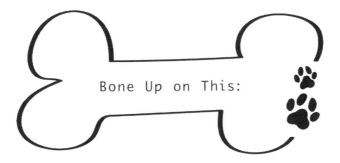

Bone Up on This:

Dear children, do not let anyone lead you astray. He who does what is right is righteous, just as He is righteous.

1 John 3:7

Father, help me to practice righteous living wherever I am and whoever I am with.

DON'T EAT POOP

I OFTEN REFUSED Molly's typical greeting—a kiss with her long, wet tongue. Molly's affectionate gestures came from the best intentions, but I knew what she ate.

Molly's former life, her months of living under a porch and not knowing when her next meal might appear, gave her interesting dietary habits. When out for a walk, Molly attempted to ingest a variety of items—sticks, plants, bones, fur, feathers, and, yes, even droppings the deer left behind.

I often grabbed her, pried open her mouth, and shook out whatever disgusting thing she was trying to swallow. Then I shouted, "No, Molly. Don't eat poop!"

Do you have a former life? The years before you belonged to Christ and made a commitment to follow Him? What do you still try to ingest? Paperbacks that don't edify? Websites you visit secretly? TV shows or movies which are questionable?

The items Molly grabbed during her walk through the field didn't nourish her, and they could have made her sick. Reading, listening, or viewing trash doesn't nourish us either. Don't make God shout at you, "Don't eat poop!"

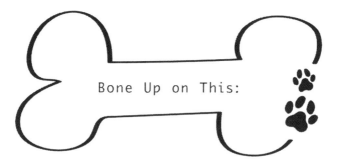

Bone Up on This:

Finally, brothers, whatever is true, whatever is noble, whatever is right, whatever is pure, whatever is lovely, whatever is admirable—if anything is excellent or praiseworthy—think about (read, listen, view) such things.

Philippians 4:8 (Author's paraphrase)

God, help me to fill my mind and soul with what is noble, right, and pure.

DEER BONES

ONE DAY, while walking in our woods, Molly found a deer bone. She considered this odoriferous object a treasure of the highest value and carried it proudly, dropping it only to take care of urgent business or to gnaw on it.

She missed all the things she usually enjoyed on our walks—racing across the field at breakneck speed, sniffing clumps of grass to see who'd been there, and even wrestling with her best friend. When she stopped to chew, she fell behind and had to run awkwardly to catch up. Yet, she refused to leave the bone.

For the next few weeks, the grimy bone was hauled to the mailbox and down the lane and back. At the house, she reluctantly obeyed my command to, "Leave it outside." But the next day she grabbed it up as soon as I opened the door.

How many of us carry "deer bones" around? Maybe it's what we say when we're angry, or an unhealthy habit. We're reluctant to put it down, sometimes even snarling at anyone who suggests we should. The bone may be nasty or offensive to others, but we're convinced it is too important to drop.

Just as Molly's deer bone didn't give her the best walking

experience, we miss out on a closer walk with God when we hold on to something we know He'd rather we leave behind.

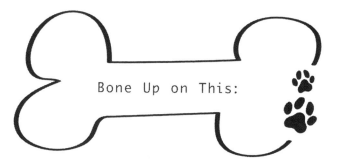

Bone Up on This:

Therefore, since we are surrounded by such a great cloud of witnesses, let us throw off everything that hinders and the sin that so easily entangles, and let us run with perseverance the race marked out for us.

Hebrews 12:1

God, help me recognize my deer bones and drop them, so I may walk freely with You.

MOVING BOXES

MOLLY'S WORLD tilted and spun out of control. We were moving from our home in the woods into a new house in the Easter Lake area of Des Moines. Gary and I frantically boxed up the contents of the home where we'd lived for twenty-eight years. And Mollie worried.

She knew packing meant changes. It could mean a camping trip. Or a vacation in the car. But it might mean we would leave her with the tall man (our adult son) who frightened her. So, she worried.

She followed me from room to room, jumped when doors opened or shut, and even licked the hair off a small area on her foot.

If Molly could understand, I would have told her, "We're moving to a place that has a LAKE. We're going to fence the yard, so you can go out whenever you want. We will still have the comfy couches, carpet, and beds. Don't be afraid. Don't worry."

But Molly couldn't understand. She trusted me, but not enough. So, she worried.

Is God moving you? Maybe not to a new house, but a new circumstance, a new season of life, or a new area of service? God tells you, *"Do not be anxious about anything." Philippians 4:6.*

Do you trust God enough, even when He moves boxes around you?

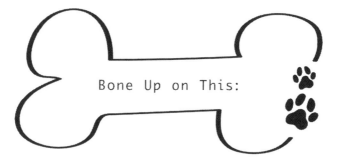

"For I know the plans I have for you," declares the Lord, *"plans to prosper you and not to harm you, plans to give you hope and a future."*

Jeremiah 29:11

God, help me to trust You always, even when my circumstances leave my world in upheaval.

LIVING REDEEMED

THE SHELTER RESCUE staff pulled Molly from the dirt under the porch. After a few weeks of vet visits and getting to know her, they put her up for adoption. We paid the fees and signed the adoption contract. Molly had been redeemed, but she had no idea how to live without the security of the hole she'd always known.

For years, we called her Crazy Molly. Strangers, loud noises, and, most of all, being caught, terrified her. When she escaped the backyard or slipped out the door, she did all she could to avoid capture, eluding us until we enticed her with food she couldn't resist. She destroyed things in our house—chewing her way through a vast assortment of items, from those of little value to a few of great value. And she never quite got over being starved. She snatched and swallowed anything edible within her reach.

When we acknowledge Jesus Christ as our Savior and Lord, He pulls us from the dirt of our own making. We are redeemed, but sometimes we are clueless about how to live outside our familiar place in the dirt.

Redemption is a daily process. Embracing new truths and rejecting old habits is hard work. We must acknowledge Jesus as our Lord every morning, continually ask forgiveness for our sins, and praise Him with gratitude for His purchase of us.

Bit by bit, after many years, Molly became a well-trained dog. And if you allow Jesus to instruct you for many years, your Master will also say, *"Well done, my good and faithful servant" (Matthew 25:21).*

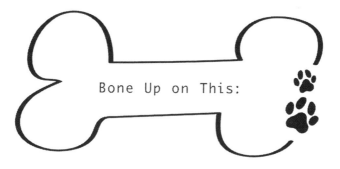

Bone Up on This:

In Him, we have redemption through His blood, the forgiveness of sins, in accordance with the riches of God's grace that He lavished on us with all wisdom and understanding.

Ephesians 1:7

God, may I ever be grateful for my redemption through Jesus Christ, Your Son.

CHOSEN
Maggie's Tale

MAGGIE'S TALE: CHOSEN

THE YOUNG COLLEGE couple didn't intend for their dogs to have a litter of puppies. He owned a male, part retriever, part beagle. She owned a female, mostly Lab. They had the male dog neutered, but no one told them the sterilization might not take effect immediately.

"It was an accident," they said when they contacted the animal shelter. "Can you find homes for them?" Ten puppies with bright eyes and curious, happy personalities won the affections of the young couple who relinquished them and the shelter workers who welcomed them.

Six months had passed since Molly's life had ended with a tumor in her nasal cavity. Despite treatment, the tumor grew and took the life of the wild girl we'd grown to love. As we grieved her loss, we spent several months spent in isolation during a pandemic and cared for our son's dogs while he underwent treatment for cancer. One day I cautiously opened Petfinder again.

I found dogs. Shaggy black dogs. Golden doodle puppies. Hound dogs with sad eyes. Five times I applied to adopt a dog. Five times we were not chosen. Each time I grew more discouraged.

Then I saw the litter of "accidents." We'd decided an older dog would be the best fit for us. A puppy had too much energy. A puppy took lots of time to train. A puppy could even outlive us.

But these dogs were partly Lab, they were available, and they needed homes. I applied to adopt without much hope we would fit their perception of good owners. I marked Angel, a nearly white puppy with floppy ears, as our choice.

Surprisingly, within a week, I received an email notifying us we'd been approved. The shelter set a date for a "meet and greet." The morning of our appointment, we drank coffee on our deck and discussed our day. Gary shook his head. "You know, this is the craziest thing we've ever done."

We drove an hour to the shelter. Our puppy, her color darkened to pale gold, entered the room—not boisterous, but confident. She greeted us, then explored the room, her nose snuffling over every inch. After a brief time of play, she stretched out for a nap. We held her, stroked her silken ears, and fell in love. We told the shelter staff we wanted her, but she needed to stay two weeks longer for vaccinations.

The two weeks became a whirlwind of preparations. We needed a crate, a place to play, a leash and collar ... so many items for a puppy. Over thirty years had passed since we'd had a young dog in the house. Could we do this?

We renamed her Maggie and picked her up on July 2. Just like any new baby, she entertained lots of visitors, especially during our annual Fourth of July cookout. Everyone held her, marveled at her huge paws, and remarked on her beauty. From the start, Maggie loved greeting people and receiving attention.

Like any new parents, the non-stop care left us exhausted, but Maggie's joyful personality more than made up for it. She knew she'd been chosen, and as she grew, she assumed an attitude of entitlement. She slept where she wanted to sleep, anything within her reach was a chew toy, and all food should be shared. We called her Lady Margaret of Evergreen by the Lake, and our house and backyard were indeed her kingdom.

By the time Maggie had her first birthday, she no longer needed constant supervision. She attended dog school and learned the basics. I took her hiking, and she became an amazing trail dog. At mealtime, she stayed in her "place" and did not beg. She knew what "not yours" and "leave it" meant. And, most of the time, she walked obediently by my side on the leash.

Our doubts slowly dissipated over the year. We could do this. Maggie had waggled her way into our hearts and lives. It may have been a crazy idea to adopt a puppy in our golden years, but it was also the perfect thing to do.

Maggie approached life with a joy like no other. Every person and every dog became an instant friend. Every new experience developed into an adventure. And she never doubted that anyone who met her, loved her, and considered her wonderful.

Maggie knew she was chosen. And we knew she'd been chosen for us.

You did not choose me, but I chose you and appointed you to go and bear fruit.

John 15:16

BITING THE LEASH

AS A PUPPY, Maggie exerted more energy than a roomful of two-year-old children. I knew she needed exercise to live calmly in the house, and I started training her on a leash shortly after she came home.

Maggie considered everything a game, and leash training was a great one. She loved following me down the sidewalk—until she wanted to go a different direction. Then she grabbed the leash in her mouth and bit, tugged, and shook it.

Maggie didn't know she needed the leash to keep her safe. She didn't know about cars in the street, or getting lost, or large, aggressive dogs. She just wanted to be free.

Sometimes, as Christians, we chafe at what we consider restrictions. We don't want to forgive, or be kind, or treat our bodies as a temple. We want to be free.

If Maggie had no leash, I would confine her to our house and backyard. She wouldn't be allowed to walk around the lake, go to a park, hike in the forest, or go camping with us in the RV. The leash frees her to go. So, biting the restraint is not helpful.

Neither is ignoring or complaining about what God has asked us to do. He has a glorious plan for our lives, and only by surrendering to Him and His path for us are we truly free.

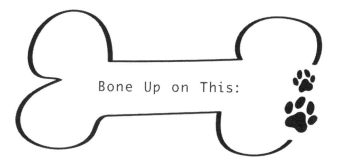

Bone Up on This:

You, my brothers, were called to be free. But do not use your freedom to indulge the sinful nature; rather, serve one another in love.

Galatians 5:13

God, help me be obedient and cheerfully follow Your directions without biting the leash.

BRIDGES AND BIG THINGS

MAGGIE HAS the appearance of a full-blooded Labrador retriever. Labs love water. I could never prevent my previous Labs from leaping into any river, lake, or even muddy ditches we passed. Maggie is much more cautious.

She learned she could get a drink from these sources, so she would daintily wade in a few steps and lap up the water. She never tried swimming. After she turned one, I encouraged her to go in farther. I threw sticks for her to fetch, I waded in myself and called her, but she would have nothing to do with any water over three inches deep.

We both love to hike the mountain bike trails at a state park near our home. The beautiful, wooded area has paths that curve steeply up the hills and down. In low spots, simple wooden bridges cross over the water from several small lakes.

One day, we hiked over a bridge spanning a run-off area. Maggie sniffed the wooden planks intently. I'm sure many critters had crossed it. One portion of the bridge slanted slightly, and Maggie, focused on her sniffing, stepped near the edge. Suddenly, all four feet went out from under her, and she slid into the water with a huge splash.

I reached down to grasp her and pull her to safety, but she swam strongly, her head high. So, I walked beside her for the few feet to the shore and showed her where she could scramble back to the path. Once out, she seemed to know she had accomplished a Big Thing. She raced up and down the trail, whirling around me, water drops cascading in her wake.

We sometimes resist what God calls us to do. Like Jonah preaching to Nineveh or Moses leading the Israelites, we make excuses, we rationalize, we think there is someone more qualified. God may let us slide off the bridge to teach us that through Him and with Him, we are able to accomplish Big Things.

If you sense God calling you to do something, pray about it, then jump into the water. God will walk beside you—and you will accomplish a Big Thing.

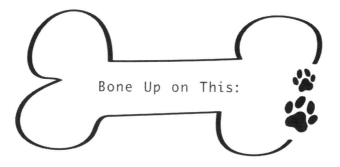

For we are God's workmanship, created in Christ Jesus to do good works, which God prepared in advance for us to do.

Ephesians 2:10

God, give me the courage to do the good works you have prepared for me.

BE GENTLE WITH THE STUFFIES

BEFORE BRINGING MAGGIE HOME, we picked out a stuffed pink puppy with floppy ears. She loved her Pink Puppy. She carried him around the house by an ear or a foot, and if we threw him for her, she skidded across the floor in pursuit. We bought her another —a soft white dog with a plastic heart that mimicked the sound of a mother dog's heartbeat. She slept with White Puppy. We found a bear and a rabbit at a garage sale. Maggie loved them all.

Then she started teething. Maggie transformed into a chewing monster. Nothing escaped the ravages of her mouth. First, Pink Puppy lost a foot. Then he was ripped open, and his stuffing deposited in fluffy piles over the family room. One by one, Maggie dismantled each stuffie. She always started with a sewn-on tag, an embroidered eye, or a tail that poked up.

I repaired them, but as soon as I handed them back to her, she'd rip a new hole. I finally gave up and piled the stuffies in a corner of my sewing closet. When I opened the door, Maggie would reach in for one of her beloved toys.

I told her firmly, "No, they're in the hospital because you bit them."

Maggie continued to mature, her teeth came in, and the chewing abated. Somewhat. I repaired the stuffies one more time and tried to teach Maggie, "Be gentle with the stuffies."

When she started to chew one, I replaced it with one of her bones. She seemed to understand. But occasionally, I still come into the room and find one of her animals torn open and the stuffing removed.

Our words have the power to tear people apart—not literally, but emotionally. And yet we criticize, give advice when it isn't welcome, and fail to encourage others. Even when the person we're discussing is absent, our words have a way of making it to them and leaving a wound. In our eyes, we see something that needs to be worked on. Like Maggie, we see a tag sticking out or a loose thread, and we just can't leave it alone and let the Holy Spirit do the convicting. We need someone to tell us, "Be gentle with the stuffies."

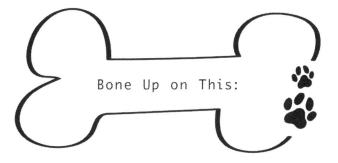

But encourage one another daily, as long as it is called Today.

Hebrews 3:13

Almighty Father, forgive me for the times I have wounded others; help me to use my words to uplift and encourage.

THE PUZZLED-PUP LOOK

"SHE'S DARLING." "What a beautiful dog." Maggie's light golden coat, big brown eyes, and floppy ears endeared her to everyone. When we spoke, she cocked her head to one side, then the other, leading me to believe she understood every word I uttered.

Yet, when I commanded her to come, or lie down, or go to "her place," she remained frozen, her head still cocked like she was trying to figure out what to do. She had learned these commands months ago, but now she acted like she'd never heard those words before. Our good friends, who kept Maggie when we were out of town, dubbed this her "puzzled-pup look." The truth is, Maggie knows exactly what we ask. She must decide if she wants to obey or not.

Sometimes I think we give God our "puzzled-pup look" when He asks us to do something. Oh, we cover our hesitations with expressions, "I need to pray about it" or "You know, the Bible isn't clear on that issue."

When God calls us to do something, like Maggie, we usually understand perfectly. But we must decide whether we will obey or not.

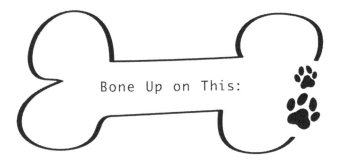

Bone Up on This:

Does the Lord delight in burnt offerings and sacrifices as much as obeying the voice of the Lord? To obey is better than sacrifice and to heed is better than the fat of rams.

1 Samuel 15:22

Although we no longer offer sacrifices, our tithes and good works can substitute in this verse. Nothing trumps obedience to God.

Father, help me to obey in all things.

WAIT WITH ANTICIPATION

MAGGIE LOVES TO LOOK OUTSIDE. In our family room, three large windows face the street. They sit about ten inches from the floor, and Maggie loves to plant her front feet on the wide windowsill. She watches the neighbors walking their dogs, children playing in their yards, and cars passing by. When something happens that really captures her interest, she presses her nose to the window. I wipe off her nose prints without scolding, knowing how much she enjoys this connection to the world beyond our house.

Maggie checks her windows throughout the day, but certain events cause greater interest. Every weekday morning during the school year, the bus stops by our house to pick up students. If we say, "Maggie, here comes the school bus," she races to the window to watch. My friend, Leigh, is a favorite of Maggie. If we say, "Leigh is coming," Maggie runs to the window. If Gary leaves in the truck, Maggie keeps her nose pressed to the window until she sees him again. She waits with great anticipation for the return of people she loves, ready to greet them with waggles and kisses.

A Friend of ours has promised His return.

This same Jesus who has been taken from you into Heaven, will come back in the same way you have seen him go into heaven.

Acts 1:11

Are we waiting for Jesus's return with our noses pressed to the window? Are we waiting in anticipation? Are we ready to greet Him with our love and praise?

What do you need to do today to be ready for Jesus's return? Is there someone you need to share the gospel with? Sin you need to confess? A broken relationship that needs mending? Do you need to spend some time in God's Word and in prayer?

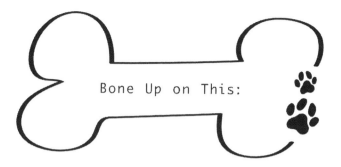

Bone Up on This:

It (the grace of God) teaches us to say "No" to ungodliness and worldly passions, and to live self-controlled, upright and godly lives in this present age, while we wait for the blessed hope—the glorious appearing of our great God and Savior, Jesus Christ.

Titus 2:12-13

Jesus, help me to prepare for your return, and to wait with anticipation.

RIVER OF DELIGHTS

WHEN MAGGIE AND I HIKE, I carry water for both of us. She has a collapsible plastic bowl that rolls up to fit in my backpack. If she's thirsty, she paws at the water bottle to ask for a drink. She waits patiently while I get her bowl and fill it. I hold it away from me because she laps with gusto, and I could end up with wet hiking pants.

But Maggie is elated when she can drink from a stream. If we hike over a bridge, she immediately turns off the path to see if there is a way down to that river of delight. Her favorite is a creek she can wade into and cool her feet as she laps the sweet nectar. She slurps and splashes and drips with no one complaining she is getting them wet. When finished drinking, she shakes the water droplets off and races down the trail. She is thoroughly refreshed.

God promised us a river of delights too.

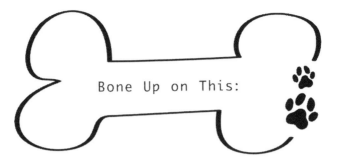

Bone Up on This:

How priceless is your unfailing love!

Both high and low among men find refuge in the shadow of your wings.

They feast on the abundance of your house;

You give them drink from your river of delights

For with you is the fountain of life; in your light we see light.

Psalm 36:7

In Isaiah, He issues the invitation:

Come, all you who are thirsty, come to the waters.

Isaiah 55:1

No matter what your status is in the world; you are invited to wade in and drink from the river of delights. Jesus told the woman at the well that He had *living water,* for He is the only source of our salvation and eternal life. God's invitation to you is to come today and be refreshed in Him.

God, help me seek out the path to Your river of delights, wade in, and drink deeply.

OFF-LEASH!

EARLY ON, I taught Maggie three different ways to accompany me outside the house. I call one "walk with me." Maggie trots by my left side, neither pulling nor lagging. This is the heel position and is required when she is in dog class or out and about with other pedestrian traffic. If Maggie had a report card, this skill would be marked *progressing,* not *proficient.*

The second one is "sniff walk." Maggie loves when I say this one. It means she can walk in the grass beside our paved trail, her nose reading the messages other critters have left. She can also stop to use the grass if she needs.

The last one is Maggie's favorite. If we are on a foot trail where it is allowed, I let Maggie go "off-leash." She dashes ahead, then turns to circle around us in an absolute frenzy of joy. As we hike, she settles in, either leading the group or stopping to explore, but always keeping within sight.

When I call Maggie, she responds, leaving her latest discovery, and trotting to my side. When we hike off-leash, she makes choices—*do I stay with my master, or do I chase the critter I hear in the woods? Do I come when she calls, or do I continue down this fascinating deer trail?*

When Maggie walks off-leash with me, she does it because she trusts I will choose the best path, and she loves me enough to stay nearby.

As we walk with God, our journeys mirror Maggie's. Sometimes God uses circumstances to keep us close to Him. Sometimes we have more choices to make, but we sense God near and know His leading. I believe, sometimes, God lets us run off-leash.

This isn't an opportunity to go as if God is not there, or to take a wrong path, or make a dangerous choice. His desire is that we will choose Him and the path He has for us.

Will you trust God enough to follow Him where He leads, even when another fascinating path beckons? Do you love Him enough to want to stay close to Him? What do you need to do today to draw near God?

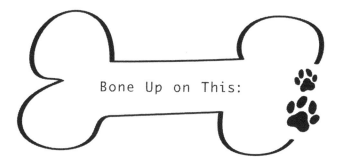

Blessed are those who have learned to acclaim You, who walk in the light of Your presence, O Lord. They rejoice in your name all day long; they exult in your righteousness.

Psalm 89:15

God, may I always choose to stay with You and walk with You on the path You have chosen.

OUTGROWING THE BED

AS A PUPPY, Maggie slept in a crate in our bedroom. When she woke and whined, I took her outside. Afterward, she settled back on her blanket. If not, a firm "Shhhh," and she would quiet. In the mornings, she often whined before we were ready to get up. If I opened the crate, she stretched and made her way around to Gary's side of the bed. She knew he would lift her up. We would each get our portion of puppy kisses, and then she snuggled down in our bed until we chose to rise.

We went on a camping trip when Maggie was six months old. She never needed to go out during the night anymore, and she was reliable during the daytime. We decided not to crate her. I made her bed on the floor from blankets. Maggie turned a few times, then settled in for the night—or so we thought. The mattress in our trailer sat closer to the floor than the one at home, and Maggie had grown quite tall. She could jump lightly onto the bed and lay down between us. If she waited until we were sound asleep, we never knew she was there. Until we tried to roll over, and a dog's paw poked us in the face.

When we returned from our trip, Maggie continued the habit. Both Gary and I liked to snuggle with Maggie, but our bed was not big enough for all of us. I fixed her a place on the floor with a cozy blanket, and we used a plastic expandable fence to keep her in it.

Maggie accepted her new area, and we all slept better.

Like Maggie, we sometimes cling to what we find comfortable. God calls us to continually mature in our faith and to leave behind what we have outgrown. What immature habits are you clutching? How do you need to grow up into Him?

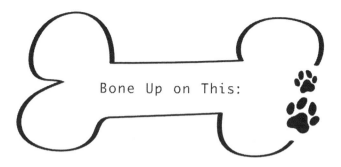

Then we will no longer be infants, tossed back and forth by the waves, and blown here and there by every wind of teaching and by the cunning and craftiness of men in their deceitful scheming. Instead, speaking the truth in love, we will in all things grow up into him who is the Head, that is, Christ.

Ephesians 4:14-15

Jesus, help me let go of what I have outgrown and grow up into You.

HIKING RULES

I OFTEN HIKE with a friend or two. Maggie loves having a group and thinks it makes the journey more fun. But she had to establish a few rules:

1. *Stay with the leader.* Maggie prefers to be at the front of the group, not the rear. If I give her the *go behind* command, she does it, but she continually pushes around to check on the leader.
2. *The group stays together.* If someone steps off the path and heads away from the group, Maggie runs between the loner and the rest of the group. If anyone restrains her, she whines. She clearly wants everyone within her circle.
3. *Every side path should be explored, even if it isn't taken.* An intersecting trail, a spur, or just a faint deer path through the vegetation—all cause Maggie to hesitate. If I say, "No, Maggie, we're going this way," she's agreeable; she just wants us to know there's an alternate route.
4. *Don't forget to stop and refresh yourself.* If we cross a creek, pass a bench, or go over a bridge, Maggie must stop for a

break. She loves to lap cool water, sit on a bench with me, or explore underneath a bridge.

5. *Go with joy.* When Maggie hikes, her exuberant joy is visible. If she's off-leash, she runs in giant circles around us, racing up and down the trail. It doesn't matter if we're climbing a difficult uphill stretch, or the sun is beating down on us, or we are so tired we can barely put one foot in front of the other, her joy never dims.

In our walk with God, we need to remember Maggie's rules:

1. *Let God lead.* Never take your eyes off Him.
2. *You need fellow Christians.* Foster relationships within your church, small group, and Christian friends. Help unite the body of Christ.
3. *Listen to God.* He may be telling you to proceed; He may be telling you to take the side path; He may be telling you to turn around.
4. *Pause often and refresh yourself in Him.*
5. *Never let your joy dim.*

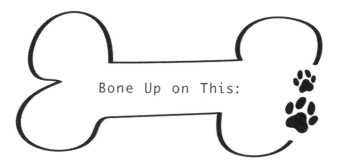

But He knows the way that I take ... My feet have closely followed His steps; I have kept to His way without turning aside.

Job 23:10-11

Oh Lord, help me follow You and only You.

CHOSEN

ALTHOUGH PEOPLE CALLED the birth of Maggie and her siblings "an accident," Maggie never felt the sting of the stigma. She seemed to know from the beginning she was chosen, and that she has a plan and a purpose.

Her plans do not always coincide with ours, as when she decided she could jump on the bed and sleep with us, but she was quick to adjust to our plan and is always joyful and loving.

When she does something wrong, she never seems bothered by discipline. Sometimes, this made it difficult to correct. I used a can of pennies to shake at her when we wanted to change a behavior. She soon learned it was just a noise and ignored it. She understands perfectly when we are upset with her, but she knows she is loved, and we will forgive.

You are not an accident either. You are part of God's plan from the beginning. He created you and has a plan for you. You are chosen.

To know we are chosen shouldn't cause arrogance or entitlement, but down-on-our-knees gratitude. We did nothing to earn God's approval, loving care, or eternal life. God gave us these gifts because He chose to rescue and redeem us.

When we do something wrong, there will be consequences. But, like Maggie, we can rejoice there is nothing we can do to diminish God's love for us. We ask and are forgiven.

Do you live like you're chosen? Are you full of gratitude? Full of joy? Do you adjust easily when God's plans and yours don't coincide?

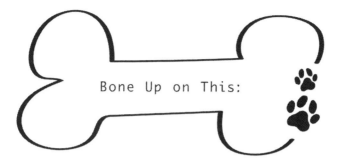

Bone Up on This:

But you are a chosen people, a royal priesthood, a holy nation, a people belonging to God, that you may declare the praises of Him who called you out of darkness into His wonderful light.

1 Peter 2:9

God, thank You for Your great love for me, and thank You for choosing me to be Yours.

AUTHOR'S NOTE

Note to my Readers:

If you believe in our Lord Jesus Christ and have trusted Him to be your Savior, you, too, are *rescued, redeemed, and chosen.*

My prayer for you is that you will live:

- like Annie—loving everyone and rescuing others
- like Molly—conforming your heart to your Master's plan
- like Maggie—filled with overflowing gratitude and joy in the knowledge of being chosen

ABOUT THE AUTHOR

Susan Lawrence is a speaker, an author, and a storyteller. She grew up on a farm in the heart of Iowa. As a child, she learned to love country life, writing stories, and her Savior, Jesus Christ.

She graduated from Kansas State Teacher's College and taught special needs children for twenty-six years before putting away the chalkboard to devote more time to writing, speaking, and storytelling.

Susan lives and travels with Gary, her husband and best friend for fifty-two years, and their rescue pup, Maggie. She has three adult children and seven brilliant and beautiful grandchildren who love to hear her stories.

When Susan is not writing, she enjoys spending time with her family, hiking in the woods, bicycling, and traveling. But most of all, she loves to tell the story, the good news of Jesus Christ, in writing, speaking, and living.

Her published works include two family devotion books; three novels, *Atonement for Emily Adams*, *Restoration at River's Edge*, and *Flight of the Red-winged Blackbird;* two middle grades novels, *The Blue Marble* and *The Long Ride Home;* a picture book, *Shepherd of eSwatini*, and her newest, *Three Dogs' Tales*. She has also contributed to three anthologies and has written many articles for various Christian publications.

ALSO BY SUSAN R. LAWRENCE

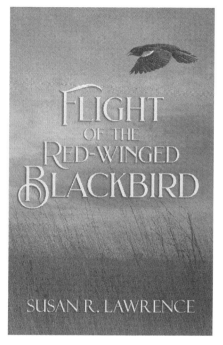

Flight of the Red-winged Blackbird

In 1932, Ruth Russo flees the farm where she arrived as an orphaned teenager and seeks refuge at Sisters of Mercy Home for unwed mothers. When the haven she hopes for becomes a place of tragedy, she flees again, and attempts to support herself in a culture of discrimination and a country burdened by the Great Depression.

Her days brighten when she reconnects with Jack, a friend from high school. But Jack is a budding lawyer, and she is a maid in his cousin's house. Will Ruth be able to lay down her burden of shame and accept love, not only from Jack, but also from God?

Get your copy here:
https://scrivenings.link/redwingedblackbird

Made in the USA
Columbia, SC
11 September 2023